The Loon
Voice of the Wilderness

The Loon
Voice of the Wilderness

CHARLENE W. BILLINGS

A SKYLIGHT BOOK

DODD, MEAD & COMPANY
New York

PHOTOGRAPH CREDITS

Photographs courtesy of: © 1981 Woody Hagge, pages 12-13, 23; © Morgan Hebard, Jr., 32-33 (top), 32-33 (bottom); F. G. Irwin, 10, 11, 15, 16, 18-19 (top), 19 (bottom), 20-21, 25, 26, 28-29, 30; N. H. Loon Preservation Committee, 8, 36, 42, 43, 44: Jack Swedberg, Massachusetts Division of Fisheries and Wildlife, 39.

Published by Dodd, Mead & Company, Inc.,
71 Fifth Avenue, New York, N.Y. 10003
Printed in The United States of America by Horowitz/Rae
Designed by Jean Krulis

1 2 3 4 5 6 7 8 9 10

Library of Congress Cataloging-in-Publication Data

Billings, Charlene W.
   The loon.
   (A Skylight book)
   Includes index.
   Summary: Follows a pair of common loons from spring mating to fall migration and discusses the survival problems facing the "great northern diver."
   1. Common loon—Juvenile literature. [1. Loons] I. Title.
QL696.G33B54   1988   598.4'42   87-27607
ISBN 0-396-09244-6

For Allen

Acknowledgments

My sincere appreciation to everyone who has shared their knowledge about loons with me for this book. Special thanks to Tom Klein for helping me to locate photographers and to Dr. F. Glenn Irwin, Woody Hagge, Morgan Hebard, Jr., Bill Byrne of the Massachusetts Division of Fisheries and Wildlife, and Jeff Fair, Director of the New Hampshire Loon Preservation Committee, for their cooperation in providing photographs and for generous offers to assist in any way. In addition, thank you to Dr. Paul I.V. Strong, Certified Associate Wildlife Biologist, Sigurd Olson Environmental Institute, Northland College, for reading the manuscript for accuracy.

Contents

Wilderness lake.

1.

Spring Arrival

Except for the music of the wind through the forest, few sounds can be heard on the North Country lake in New Hampshire. It is early May. Reflections of spruce, balsam, fir, and white birch trees shimmer on the sunlit surface of the water.

One day, just before dusk, a pair of birds flies in wide circles over the lake, then splash down on the water. They are common loons *(Gavia immer)*. Spine-tingling cries pierce the stillness.

"A-a-whoo-quee-quee-whe-oooo-que!"

"A-a-whoo-quee-quee-whe-oooo-que!"

The male repeats the call again and again to claim up to one hundred acres or more of this untamed territory for himself and his mate. The strange, eerie voice of the loon has made this bird the symbol of the northern wilderness areas of the United States and Canada for as long as there has been anyone to hear it. To the ancient ancestors of the Crees and other Indian tribes, these were the cries of restless spirits.

Male and female loons look alike. Each one is around

A pair of adult loons in the water.

Close-up of a loon's head.

thirty inches long and weighs about ten pounds, about the same size as a small goose. Square-shaped white markings on the black feathers of their backs and upper wings make a checkerboard pattern. Their heads and necks look as if they are made of black velvet that glistens with green highlights. Their necks are adorned with a collar of white lines and they wear a chinstrap of short

11

white lines. Breasts and undersides are white as snow.
Both birds have sturdy, dark, dagger-shaped bills and
ruby red eyes.

The loons have flown a long distance from their winter
home on the ocean. They have returned to this cool, deep
lake to raise a family.

The pair swims and dives with powerful legs and large
webbed feet. One soon surfaces with a fish and swallows
it headfirst. Within seconds the bird dives again. The pair
continue this until they have eaten their fill. Sometimes
they catch frogs, insects, leeches, or crayfish as well as
fish.

Loon with a catch of fish.

Loons are experts at diving and swimming. For this reason, some people also call loons "great northern divers." But as much as loons are at home in the water, they are almost helpless on land. They cannot walk in a normal manner. They shuffle and slide on their breasts, sometimes using their wings to help themselves move. Their legs are too far back on their bodies to support them properly. This awkwardness afoot may be the source of their name. Loon is from an old English word "lumme," which means a lummox or clumsy person.

2.

Raising a Family

The loons spend a week or more resting and fishing.

Then, one day, the male and female swim toward each other dipping their beaks and flicking sprays of water. They toss their heads. Their excitement builds and the two birds dive together many times—slicing through the water at several miles per hour. To end their courtship display, the pair preen their feathers with their bills— smoothing and grooming each one.

After courting, the male follows the female onto land to mate. Loons usually return to the same area to breed each year and may have only one partner for life. This pair has been returning to this lake for six years.

Loon dance.

Within days, the birds seek a place to nest. This time they choose the same site as last year. The remains of the old nest are on the very edge of a small island in the lake. This nesting spot surrounded by water is safer than the one on the shore of the mainland that the pair used in earlier years. It is less likely to be found by hungry animals.

Now only a day away from laying her eggs, the female gathers mud from the bottom of the lake, as well as reeds, leaves, sticks, moss, and grass. Her mate helps. Together, they form these coarse materials into a shallow hollow about two feet across, big enough to hold an adult loon.

Once the nest is ready, the female lays one olive-brown speckled egg. Two days later, she lays a second egg to complete her clutch.

Two eggs on the nest.

Both parents take turns sitting on the eggs, the incubating duties shared equally by male and female. The eggs must be kept warm or they will not hatch. Also, the eggs are in danger of being eaten by enemies whenever left unattended. Mink, muskrats, foxes, otters, skunks, or raccoons may destroy the nest. Birds such as gulls and crows steal loon eggs if given the chance. Fortunately, the mottled coloration of the eggs may make them difficult for enemies to see. And the watchful adults seldom leave the nest at the same time.

The parent birds take turns egg-sitting, so that each one can swim and eat. When either bird returns to the nest, it gently rolls the eggs over and rearranges the grass and twigs a bit with its bill before settling down. This keeps the eggs evenly warm.

After twenty-eight days the chicks are cheeping faintly within their shells. With their beaks they peck and peck for hours at the shells that hold them captive. At last, one of the shells cracks and splits open. A loon chick struggles out—exhausted, wet, and sticky.

As a steady cold drizzle starts to fall, the mother loon

Adult loon on the nest in an alert position.

Just hatched. Close-up of adult loon with newly hatched chick under its body.

tucks the newcomer under her wing. In this warm, protected place, the chick's thick down of fine feathers dries and becomes soft and fluffy. Its head, back, and upper wings are sooty black, but its undersides are pale gray.

Two days later, as the weather clears, the second egg hatches.

Like barnyard chicks, the hungry hatchlings peep constantly for their parents' attention.

Two adult loons in the water with young.

Within hours of hatching, the second loon chick's down is dry and fluffy. After twelve hours or more, both chicks leave the nest with their mother and father. They toddle and tumble into the water. Off they swim, stroking first with one tiny webbed foot and then the other. Once in a while, they duck their heads underwater. If they try to dive, they bob up like corks because air trapped in their fluffy down keeps them afloat. The adults stay nearby and bring their youngsters small fish. The loon chicks swallow the fish right away.

Within a few days, the loon chicks preen instinctively,

without being taught. Like their parents and other birds, each one forces oil out of glands at the base of its tail with its beak. Each small bird strokes the oil onto its downy feathers to make them waterproof. The well-oiled feathers are like a raincoat that keeps out water, so that the loon's body stays warm and dry.

The youngsters flutter their tufts of tails and flap their wings to shed droplets of water and to fluff their feathers. Often, mother or father offers them shelter under a wing.

Especially during the first few weeks of life, danger lurks in the depths of the lake for the young loons. On the fourth day an old snapping turtle strikes at one of the chicks. It barely misses snatching a tiny paddling foot. Before it can try again, the young loon climbs upon its mother's back. Young loons often ride piggyback on their parents for protection, as well as rest and warmth. When the parents tire of this, they simply ruffle their feathers or dive underwater to push the young ones off.

By the time one week has passed, the chicks have learned to dive to depths up to ten feet and to catch a few fish. Their parents continue to feed them too, however.

When the chicks are one week old, a powerboat roars

Young loon riding piggyback.

over the lake. The male loon gives a warning call. But it is too late! The driver of the boat carelessly cuts between one of the chicks and the rest of the loon family. The frightened lone chick paddles desperately toward some reeds to get away. A Northern pike swoops up. In an instant the large fish swallows the small loon.

With quivering wings, the parent loons hastily guide their only chick nearer to the shore, as the sound of the boat fades.

When the chick is three weeks old, another male loon appears in the next cove of the lake one morning. The father loon wastes no time. He sinks silently from sight and resurfaces nearer the cove. He sounds his territorial *yodel*.

"*A-a-whoo-quee-quee-whe-oooo-que!*"

"*A-a-whoo-quee-quee-whe-oooo-que!*"

As he crosses the water to confront the intruder, the father loon thrashes the water with his wings. Nearing the other bird, he stretches up, treads the surface of the water with his feet, and spreads his wings, to make himself appear large and frightening.

The female loon is startled by the fuss. She stays near her chick. But she voices long, penetrating *wails* that can be mistaken for the haunting howls of a wolf.

"*Ahaa-ooo-oooo-ooo-ahh.*"

Faced with this aggressive defense, the single male loon cries out in a *tremolo*—a weird, unearthly sound that is like the laughter of a madman. He rises up out of the

An adult rising up out of the water.

water and "rows" across the surface flapping his wings in swift retreat with the father loon still chasing him. Over and over he gives the tremolo call and then takes flight. He does not return.

During nesting time and while raising their youngster, the loons use several calls. Besides their yodel, tremolo, and wail, the loons and their chick "talk" to each other with gently voiced staccato *hoots*. The hoots are not loud, but sometimes they can be heard up to a mile away. The loon family also makes sounds like "*kuk*" or "*gek-gek*."

Loon vocalizing. Note the puffed throat.

3.

Winter on the Ocean

For five or six weeks the young loon is covered with soft down. But as it matures, much of its down is gradually replaced by brownish-gray feathers. The shedding or *molting* takes several weeks. The young bird will keep its new plumage nearly one year. The parent birds molt in the fall. Gray-and-white winter plumage takes the place of their black-and-white feathers.

When ten to twelve weeks old, the young loon tries to fly. It flaps its wings and scampers along the water's surface. Day after day, it practices running into the wind until its wingbeats are strong and it races over the water

An adult loon in the water with a half-grown chick.

with sure, long strides. By early fall, the young bird succeeds in taking off. Now that it can fly, the young loon is a *fledgling*.

In the crisp dawn of fall mornings, the parent loons join in chorus with the calls of other loons on distant

lakes. After breeding season, the birds no longer protect their territory. Their yodels, wails, and tremolos are greetings to each other. A small group of adult loons and a few fledglings gather on the lake.

During cold fall nights, ice crystallizes along the edge

Adult loon stretching.

of the water. It glitters in the sunrise and does not melt. In a few weeks, the lake will freeze over completely. Alone, or in twos or threes, the adult loons take off. They fly south toward their winter home on the open ocean. The fledglings may wait for another week or more before flying southward.

Birds follow a well-known route called a *flyway*. A flyway includes the birds' nesting areas in the North, their winter home farther south, and all the stopping places where they rest and feed while traveling.

There are four major flyways in North America that are used by millions of migrating birds. The Central and Mississippi flyways are routes over the interior part of our continent. The Atlantic and Pacific flyways are routes along our East and West coasts. Loons flying south from New England probably migrate along the Atlantic flyway, but very little is actually known about loon migration. Some believe that loons stay close to large bodies of water and fly by the shortest route to the ocean.

The loons usually fly by day along the coast. Sometimes they are as far out to sea as twenty miles or as

Adult loon flying low over the water.

Loon taking off.

high up as one thousand feet. At other times they fly closer to shore and at a lower elevation.

The loons fly with their heads and necks lower than their backs. Thus they appear hunchbacked in the air. Their feet trail behind their short tail feathers. Their churning wingbeats are rapid, strong, and uninterrupted. They fly at speeds of sixty miles per hour or more.

Whenever they are hungry and tired, the loons stop to swim and fish near the seacoast. Other small groups of loons occasionally join them to rest and feed.

The greatest gatherings of wintering loons on the Atlantic Ocean are off the coasts of North Carolina, Virginia, and Maryland. More studies are needed, however, before scientists can know the destination of individual loons.

Loons fly to ocean wintering grounds anywhere off the coast from Newfoundland to the Gulf of Mexico, Trinidad, the Bahamas, and the northern coast of South America. Loons in the Pacific area winter off the coast from California to Alaska.

4.

Northward Bound

In early spring, the adult loons molt. Once again their drab winter plumage is replaced with striking black-and-white feathers. Soon they are ready to start their journey northward to their breeding grounds. They time their flights to arrive just after the ice melts. The male and female loon may not spend the winter on the ocean together, but during their life-spans of fifteen to thirty years, the pair return each spring to the same lake. Often the male arrives a day or two earlier than his mate.

The loons' offspring probably remains on the ocean with other young loons for the next two or three years,

Ice-out. View of a northern lake just after ice-out.

until it is old enough to have chicks of its own. Then, it too will seek a mate and fly to the breeding grounds in the north.

The breeding range of common loons covers most of Canada, the southern edges of Iceland, and most of Alaska (including the Alaskan peninsula and Aleutian Islands). It also includes the northern states of Maine, New Hampshire, Vermont, New York, Michigan,

Wisconsin, and Minnesota. Massachusetts, Montana, Washington, Wyoming, and North Dakota have small numbers of breeding loons.

"*A-a-whoo-quee-quee-whe-oooo-quee!*"

An unforgettable, wild voice pierces the night air.

"*Ahaa-ooo-oooo-ooo-ahh!*"

A wolflike wail is sounded in reply. The loons have returned to their North Country lake to raise another family.

5.

New Dangers, New Hope

All along the southern edge of its breeding range in the United States, the number of common loons has dwindled in the past fifty years. The increased use of ponds and lakes for recreation in these areas is one major reason for this. As people build more summer cottages, and more powerboats arrive to disturb the loons, fewer and fewer of these birds return.

Also, raccoons truly have become "masked bandits" to breeding loons. The very presence of people has driven out the natural enemies of the raccoon. In addition, these animals thrive on the garbage people leave behind. Thus, where there were no raccoons twenty years ago, hundreds now live. In 1978, Vermont reported that raccoons destroyed one out of three of the loon nests in that state. In New Hampshire, about one-half of all loon nests suffered the same fate.

The loons' winter home also is threatened. There is a new and unnatural peril on the ocean wintering

A raccoon—predator of the loon.

grounds—fuel oil spills. A spill need not be large to be deadly. Once fuel oil coats a bird's feathers, the bird is in grave danger. This kind of oil soaks into the bird's plumage and destroys its ability to keep out the damp and cold. The loon swallows the oil when it preens as well. Even in small amounts, it slowly destroys the stomach, liver, and other parts of the body. Since young loons probably spend their first three years at sea, the threat to them is even greater than to migrating adults. Also, during molts at sea the birds cannot fly away from a spill.

Another recent problem that endangers loons is *acid rain*. When moisture in the air combines with certain fumes from industrial smokestacks, acid rain is produced. Acid rain contains harsh, corrosive chemicals. Winds can carry acid rain to distant locations before it falls to earth. As harmful chemicals gradually accumulate in a lake, fish and other forms of life in the water die. Then the loons have nothing to eat. Already, acid rain has polluted nine out of ten Adirondack lakes above two thousand feet, according to a study by Cornell University. Such lakes are soon without the song of the loon.

In several northern states in the United States now,

there are groups of people who are working to help the loon. Many of these people are volunteers who work without pay.

Artificial islands made of logs covered with sedges, twigs, and sphagnum moss are being anchored in open water to encourage nesting in some states. The loons seem content to use these. The nests built on these "islands" are safer from land predators than those along the mainland.

On some lakes, warning floats are put into place to show boaters where there are active nesting sites. Thus people can avoid accidentally disturbing the loons while the birds are raising their young.

Educational programs, signs, posters, and information displayed in public places are making more people aware of the plight of the loon and the need to protect this threatened bird.

Sometimes the fragile balance of life or death for an individual loon can be tipped toward survival.

One July, severe rains separated a pair of parent loons and one chick from their nest along the shore of Lake Winnipesaukee. The nest still contained one unhatched

Volunteers building an artificial nesting island for loons.

egg, however. The day after the storm, the adult birds did not return. But the lone egg hatched into a peeping baby loon!

The chick was discovered by a volunteer who had been watching the nest for the New Hampshire Loon Preservation Committee.

Two loon eggs on a nest built on an artificial raft. Two eggs are the usual clutch size.

With the cooperation of local CB radio buffs, members of the Committee (who call themselves the Loon Rangers) began to search for the newly hatched chick's lost family. Meanwhile, the small loon was placed in a box lined with an old coat. In a short time, the volunteers

43

Baby loon being floated off on a boat cushion to rejoin its family.

found the parent loons and one chick in a nearby cove of the lake.

But could the loon chick be introduced to its family successfully? Would the parents accept as their own this chick they had never seen?

From a boat, a Committee member floated the loon chick into the water on a life cushion. The adult loons

44

heard it peeping. Without hesitating, they wailed in reply and swam to claim their chick.

The reunion was a triumph!

To those in many states who work to help the loon, every effort made to save this enchanting bird is worthwhile. Their hope is to preserve a place for the loon on the northern lakes in the United States that it has come home to for countless springs. To them, the loon is the voice of the wilderness.

Index